PERCEPTIONS

A Collection of Poems

John Lloyd Jones

Perceptions : A Collection of Poems

ISBN 1-84426-346-0

First Published 2005 by.
UPFRONT PUBLISHING LTD
Peterborough, England.

Printed by Copytech UK Ltd.

iv

John Lloyd Jones, born March 1946 Highgate London, the son of a Yorkshire-born Methodist Minister.

After retiring from his Insurance Business in London he spent some time living in the Highlands of Scotland subsequently moving to the Yorkshire Dales, this is where he started to write poetry.

Many of his poems are based on very personal experience.

He is involved with voluntary and charitable work in North Yorkshire and London.

Now living in the heart of Wensleydale in a rural farmhouse with his partner Karen and their three dogs, Henry, Buttons and Mac.

John is affectionately known as "J.J."

Perceptions *is* a wonderfully emotive
collection of poems with observations
on humour, language, spirituality and love,
to the horrors of self-harm, alcoholism,
mental illness and suicide.

John Lloyd Jones captures experience
with feeling, vividly, in this his first book.

The cover photograph shows
J.J. at Cobo Bay, Guernsey, C.I.

Appreciation

My love and heartfelt thanks to Karen, life partner, companion, friend, teacher, toughest editor and most loyal supporter — a blessing in my life.

Dedication

This book is dedicated with ever
loving affection to my sons

DAVID and SIMON

Contents

	Page
Perceptions	3
Farmhouse Table	4
Stop	5
Goodwill	6
Pace	7
Computer	8
Bad Dream	9
Now	10
Walking Stick	11
Smell	12
She	13
Weep Not	14
Valentine's Day	15
Reach	16
First Shoot	17
Weather	18
Absorb	19
Hunter	20
How Did They Die?	21
Fat Farmer's Dogs	22
Wonder	23
Second Life	24
Stillness	25
Not Blasphemous	26
Flame	27

	Page
Awakening	28
Faith	29
Heavenly	30
This Life	31
Praise	32
Gratitude	33
All That Is	34
Things	35
Truth	36
Calendar	37
Friends	38
Sister	39
1st January	40
Ruth	41
P.C.	42
Superstition	43
Lotto	44
Beyond	45
Cockney Speak	46
Translation	47-48
Adapt	49
Smoke	50
Haircut	51
Television	52
Walk	53
Day Off	54-55
Motorway	56
Broad Yorkshire Speak	57

	Page
Ford Consul	58
What A Life	59
Sunday Lunch	60
A Short Phone Call	61
Despair	62-63
Piano Lessons	64
Hazel	65
Care	66
Joining Forces	67
Down And Out	68
Tears Of Joy	69
Jeff	70
Just A Few Words	71
AA	72
Bewilderment	73
Charles	74-75
Self Help	76
What Is The Problem?	77
Neighbour	78
Unheard	79
Shopper	80
Hereafter	81
Equal	82
Outcast	83
Winner	84
Book Of Life	85
Dress Sense	86
Presents	87

	Page
Christmas Shopping	88
Artist	89
Listen	90
Hope	91
Love	92
Gifts	93
Unseen	94
Love's Clock	95
No Lies	96
Changes	97
United	98
Forever Love	99
Yesterday	100
Wish	101
Benevolence	102
Killing	103
Life Span	104
Day And Night	105
With Love	106
Unspoken	107
No Matter	108
Cecilia	109

PERCEPTIONS

A Collection of Poems

John Lloyd Jones

Perceptions

Become aware of though our senses
Recognise as we observe
Daily happenings, events and people
Let none of these us unnerve

Comprehend we try to grasp
Misunderstandings may then end
Perceive, have insight, intuition
Heartache, worry, all will transcend.

JJ

Farmhouse Table

Almost two hundred years old measuring 8` x 4`, used daily
Abused, initials carved, hearts, many ring marks, knives dropped
Spaniels, setters gnawing, biting legs, evidence remains

Grouse, pheasants, rabbits, blood soaking through pine
Sodden clothes, guns, cartridges, boots, bags, caps
Ale, tobacco, ash, socks, matches, pipes, feet, food

Recently the owner died, all contents of the house were put to auction
The catalogue showed the table sized in metres, it was sold
Now in a penthouse apartment at Canary Wharf

Hardly ever used, a cleaner comes in twice weekly
Beeswax is so pungent all blemishes now obliterated
The new owners are delighted with their purchase
What a talking point – how they love telling stories.

JJ

Stop

Trains rush over level crossings
Aircraft criss-cross the sky
Ships navigating the ocean
Trucks, cars, speeding
Elevators moving fast

People, all hurry
This is a carousel
This is a merry-go-round
This is a life

Unable to continue
Must step off
Must stand down
Need to end
STOP.

JJ

Goodwill

Free parking the sign read, three hundred spaces
It was December 23rd a huge supermarket
He'd driven around three or four times, no available spaces
Someone then starts to pull out, at last he thought

Reversing up to the space, just about to turn
A car from the other direction drives straight in behind him
He jumps out of his car and remonstrates with this driver
I've been round and round, fifteen minutes I've been here, this is my place

"Tough, it's mine now mate," he says, and walks off

I always try and shop early at Christmas time.

JJ

Pace

Pace in changing times
Go with the flow
Keep it going
Mobile 'phone, six months old, change it

Flat screen T.V. one year old
Now Plasma, can be hung on the wall
Pace, change, keep it going

Video recorder — obsolete
LP records — gone
Pace, change, keep it going

New car today
New model tomorrow
Keep up with the changes
Keep the pace going

My friend starts a new job today
Working in a paper-less office
Pace, change, keep it going.

J J

Computer

Processing data to a set of instructions
Old thoughts, some new fill the mind, mental images
Recycled thoughts, others deleted then retrieved, thoughts saved
No megabytes or kilobytes, no hard or floppy disk
Keypad, mouse, flat screen and tower, none required
Hold fast, think straight, always on line, thoughts in the mind.

JJ

Bad Dream

Gloom enshrouded the old house it looked silent and bereft
A winged leather chair in the corner of one room
With a cushion, was all that was left

The house was cold and empty, the roof leaked, it was damp
Looking up through the window I glimpsed the keeper with a lamp
Was this the return journey that the occupant had made
Or yet another vision the old country house displayed

Stories that were once told now seemed to come to life
The past is now the present, please let there be no strife
Good cheer and joy is what I ask from this man seen tonight
Do happy greetings now await, I see his welcome light

The man approached so silently, knocking gently at the door
When opened he said softly I've passed this way before
In fact I used to live here some 300 years ago, the year was 1721
I'll now stay and never go

Was this a dream, a vision, was this real I could not tell
The man then lifted from the ground was this heaven or was it hell
He floated silently across the room and reached the leather chair
Swaying gently back and forth, seizing hold his hair

His scream was piercing it went through me like a spear
My heart it pounded, throbbing loud
Mind and body filled with fear
Please let this dream end I begged
I can go on no more, is this the end, finality
Leave now, for evermore.

Now

Lunch over, jobs to be done, why now?
Can they be left 'til later? I hear the dogs barking
They need to be walked, I will take them now

Now, now, everything now, must be done, can't wait
Is the past forgotten? The time to come unknown? Is now the future?
Grass to be cut, weeds to be pulled, trees to be pruned, right now
Car to be washed the drive must be swept now
Phone calls to make, a lamp bulb to change, the vacuum bags full right now
Must get to the shops before they close, must do it now

Should I let the dogs bark, let the grass grow, let the weeds take over now
Let the trees overhang, leave the car and the drive, leave it all now
Leave the phone calls and the vacuum, the lamp bulb can wait
The shops well tomorrow will do

Whatever I do at this precise moment in time.

J J

Walking Stick

Whose hands have held tenderly, tightly, clutching
Warm, cool, hot, cold, hands have relied upon, trusted
Move forward, ever helping, a constant companion

Silver top, worn, nurtured into misshapen images, shining bright some black
The staff of life, is this our daily bread
The infirm, or a weary traveller may disagree

Crossing paths unknown ascending stairs, laid down gently at the bedside.
Maybe reached for in the night, always ready
Dawn breaks, there to aid throughout this new day.

JJ

Smell

Hot tar, lavender, the sea, fresh bread
Smells from young days, noticed, inhaled, enjoyed
No effort
Dad's pipe tobacco

Today not easily perceived
A rose, an orchid, French perfume

Poignant times, conjured up from childhood

J J

She

She didn't ring or even text me
Left me waiting in the rain
For thirty minutes I just stood there
She'll not do this to me again

She said last Thursday that she loved me
But full commitment she could not give
She said we're good together
Right now though my heads a sieve

She said her ex: of just twelve months
Had been in touch the other day
And to her house he would be calling
Threatened, saying, I'm going to stay

She didn't ring or even text me
Left me standing in the rain
For thirty minutes I just stood there
She'll not do this to me again.

JJ

Weep Not

I cried no tears, no sorrow, no anguish
Just memories sweet in my thoughts languish

Stayed all day sat in her chair
In my mind fingers run through golden hair
Unable to happen, this now cannot be
She has gone forever, not again will I see
Alas, won't return, my heart it doth weep
No longer to lay with me, never to sleep

I cried no tears, no sorrow, no anguish
Just memories sweet in my thoughts languish.

JJ

Valentine's Day

Express love and affection to ones sweetheart
Send a gift with a card anonymously
Receive a gift and a card in the same manner

Meet for dinner at eight, both expressing surprise
Real joy, pure pleasure, delight heartfelt thanks
Expressions, feelings suddenly change

He didn't send Christian Dior Perfume
She didn't send a heart shaped card

Why this anonymity?

(St. Valentine, 3rd century AD Christian Martyr)

J J

Reach

Unattainable you are but that doesn't stop me
Transmitting thoughts of happiness towards you
I hear you on the radio, see you on T.V.
Have read your book many times, you feel part of me

We have never spoken; you're unaware that I exist
I listen, I read, I watch you, my ideal feminist
Affection with a little love I spread out for you each day
No man, they say is an island, I feel cast away.

JJ

First Shoot

The day had arrived, Richards first shoot
Several birds he expected to execute
Up high on the moor grouse beginning to fly
Gun to his shoulder, shots blast, grouse die

Richard loves this sport; he's having such fun
Bends down once again to re-load his gun
Looks ahead sees a bird with one wing badly shattered
Stamps his boot on it hard, that's all that mattered

The glorious 12th.

JJ

Weather

Days are so short
Weather is rough
They say we are in
For some heavy white stuff

Wind's really howling
Rain's coming down
Will the sun shine again?
Get rid of the frown

This feeling's called S.A.D.
Do we really know?
Oh yes, they were right
Look here comes the snow

Can't wait for the Spring
Sure we'll all feel much better
Get that warm sunny feeling
Abandon the sweater.

JJ

Absorb

Old beck you're empty, stones glisten on your bed
The gill ever flowing from a spring down hill to meet you
Clear fresh pure water underneath you moves forward

With rain your bed is covered a metre maybe more
Rocks and stones also move, small fish are seen
A heron flying overhead huge wingspan glides down

Rabbits by the waters edge, above a hawk is seen
Hanging in the air ready to drop, to kill
The unmistakable sound of a curlew is heard

Two oyster catchers seen playing
Pheasants, six or seven of them waddle along
Now taking off, they seem so clumsy.

J J

Hunter

He came with his ferrets his net and his gun
A baseball bat slung over his shoulder
Catching rabbits, for a "bit of sport" he said
The bat's often better than the gun; don't really want to fill them with lead

Without shot the butcher will take them from me
Seventy five pence each he gives
The meat's tender, really tasty, a bit pink
You'd enjoy it, in a pie, or a stew

Three ferrets he had, cream coloured
Placed them into the rabbit burrows and walked away
Now covering other burrows in the field with his nets
One of the nets suddenly appears to be moving, over he runs

Holding the bat high above his head, whoosh it comes down
An almighty thud – blood splatters his coat
"I've only been here ten minutes, not bad eh!" he says
I wish him good day, and walk back home

Later that day a knock at my door, there he stands
Fourteen I've got, would you like a couple?
The blood still dripping from the bundle of rabbits tied around his bat
I decline the offer.

J J

How Did They Die?

Was it feral cats?
May have been crows
Carrion scattered on the hill
How did they die?
Surely not foxes
No flesh would remain
Maybe a few bones
How did they die?

JJ

Fat Farmer's Dogs

Why are his dogs always tied up on a lead?
Does he think of them now and again?
Big fat farmer, he seems never in need
Why are his dogs always tied up on a lead?
Dogs crying for sustenance, needing their feed
I pray that his dogs will suffer no pain
Why are his dogs always tied up on a lead?
Does he think of them now and again?

JJ

Wonder

What men laid down these dry stone walls reaching up the hill?
The walls remain a shrine to them, some laid down their lives
Teams of men where did they live, two hundred years ago
In sheds in fields, sheltered in the Dale

Barns now converted into homes, walls three feet thick
Firm to remain in splendour
Criss-cross through the Dales magnificent walls are seen

In fields stone barns, who were these men, whence did they come,
Were wages paid, by whom?
To us a legacy. No more these skills perceived
See now the stone, exquisite, ever to abide

Wonder.

JJ

Second Life

Whatever the outcome of death let us fly
Toward this earth's ever beckoning sky
Up through the suns bright golden shaft
Does time stand still both here and aft

When this life has finally drained away
Can we now rest in a somewhat dissimilar way?
A way yet unknown to our mortal soul
Or is immortality now our new goal

If given to us, so let it be
We are unable to feel, touch, hear, smell or see
Also unsure on this second life journey
That our Angels will guide us to the next life securely

Oh that we knew our future was safe
In the Heavens above we will not disgrace
Ourselves or others whom have gone before
We pray to the Angels please grant life evermore.

JJ

Stillness

Hear the drone of the traffic trucks going up hill
Can we ever be silent? Can we ever be still?
The mind it does wonder, as we know that it will
Can we bring it back gently back to the still?

Hear radios' blaring car alarms sound so shrill
Can we ever be silent? Can we ever be still?
Let all tensions go, put bodies at rest
So our minds will not wander of this can we be blessed

Can we ever be silent? Can we ever be still?
Contemplate, focus, do our minds have their own will?
Our breathing, our thinking, should we try to let go
Say nothing, ask nothing — let stillness flow.

JJ

Not Blasphemous

God Knows! Christ Almighty!
If God knows, perhaps He'll see to it
Infinitely powerful, perhaps Christ will too
The Holy Spirit, within and around us
Divine Status.

JJ

Flame

Rekindle the fire glows dim, baskets empty, cold
Collect logs, now safely in, logs once fence posts
The rings denoting years soon to go forever
Warmth, flames, logs burning sap drips

Like molten gold flames red blue, darting flickering
Shapes like memories changing seeing faces
Thoughts of past times or what the future holds
Hopes, dreams, plans will they remain, be fruitful?

Or like the flame, the burning logs become ash and are no more
Refill the basket, stoke up the fire, the logs an endless supply
Aspirations like the logs shall burn within, they will not die
Flames burn bright hopes to ignite, this flame shall burn forever
Inextinguishable within.

J J

Awakening

Awake my heart awake my soul
No longer struggle to reach that goal
God's love, his hand now guiding me
Over life's often tempestuous sea

What goal, what is it we are trying to reach?
To some it is laying on a warm sandy beach
To others they must reach the top of their tree
Is the goal life hereafter for you and for me?

The awakening I've had is profound, it is good
I know that I'm now in some great Brotherhood
The joy, the goodwill all around me I see
Kindness, happiness, with faith, naturally

We can all look forward with God's love, tender care
One thing is for certain; we all will get "there"
Our soul, very spirit looking down from above
On all those we cherish, we can fill with our love.

J J

Faith

Believe, believe, the Minister told his congregation
And you will be saved

Saved, saved from what, danger, harm
Will no car hit us, will the aeroplane not crash

The cancer go into remission, the arthritis no longer gives pain
Our children always to be safe

Does saved mean spiritual salvation
Is this an SOS?

Who knows?

J J

Heavenly

Stairway to Heaven with steps far too high
A stairway that's wide and so long
Must we die to reach that first step?
Or in life do we just plod along?

Not to judge, be kind, do good deeds
Will this help us get on that first tread?
I've heard tell that Heaven's on earth, can this be
When we're on to those stairs we'll be dead

Have we judged, been unkind, done bad things?
Will this stairway go down to the cellar?
Join the devil in hell, fire with brimstone as well
As foretold by an old story-teller

He told me that Heaven and hell
Both do happen on earth, quite often
Seek forgiveness and show true remorse
All bad things will then be forgotten

If all is as simple as that, there's no problem
Just forgive, say sorry, apologise
Sounds so easy, does this mean we'll all go
Up those stairs, up to Heaven, to the skies?

J J

This Life

God's uplifting hand will guide us
Through the intricate maze of this life
His all seeing eye watches o'er us
His love, His kindness is rife

We thank Him, we praise Him, we bless Him
As He blesses us every day
Let us speak of Him to all and sundry
Tell all that He shows us the way

In sorrow and in happy times
God's love is always steadfast
Gives us courage and strength every day
His love forever will last

His abundant glorious love
Given freely to all, we accept
Throughout this life He cares for each one
His love carries on to the next.

J J

Praise

O God our Creator we praise thee
For all gifts sent down from above
We know Thou art watching us safely
Touching all with Thy bounteous love

Sometimes it's hard to keep going
But the strength that Thou gives to us all
You're watching o'er each one of us
With your love we know we wont fall

Our faith Lord each day getting stronger
In you Lord we place all our trust
To fight the good fight and the battles
We know your love to us all is robust

We sing praises and hallow Thy name
Ask forgiveness whenever we've sinned
Please continue to send love and light
And please Lord may it never be dimmed

Thy Kingdom O Lord it will come
Thy will O Lord will be done
When in Heaven we meet each one will we greet
All filled with your inexhaustible love.

JJ

Gratitude

Waiting in silence for God, for the Holy Spirit
Meditate and ponder, waiting in the stillness
A silent voice then speaks to me of love for all
I am filled with this goodness, with such plentiful love

This is the Holy Spirit — please God may it last
I am a seeker of the truth, of the light
Sometimes I find that which was lost
I am rewarded; I give heartfelt and grateful thanks.

JJ

All That Is

I know you are there in times of sorrow
In times of need, when all seems bad

I know you are there in times of joy
In times of plenty, when all seems good

I know you will be with me always — I know

JJ

Things

All things being equal
An eccentric saying – does it ever apply?
Consider the sun, stars, the ocean
Green fields, trees, the sky

Material things - an object
A thought, a word or deed
Our own belongings – called things
Equality indeed

A person or an animal
Regard in pity or contempt
Maybe with love, affection
Things – change the course of events

A separate entity – a thing
Of this we can be sure
Does this mean everything's a thing?
But equal – sounds too obscure.

JJ

Truth

Grass	Green
Sky	Blue
Fire	Hot
Love	True

Grass	Brown
Sky	Grey
Fire	Dies
Love	Dismay

Grass	Hay
Sky	Pink
Fire	Out
Love	Stink

JJ

Calendar

The candle burns its wax to melt
Ends with nothing — where did it go
Like thoughts, ideas, plans, disappear

Into thin air or placed elsewhere in memory in our soul
Not to forget but to return old thoughts to reach our goal
Next week, next month, next year, who knows how long we wait
Time, space, we can't define, it is an open gate

An entrance to this gate it leads to where is yet unknown
We shall reach it at some time, eternity our home
The calendar of life is marked with days with months with years
How long the days will last who knows, should we allay our fears?

JJ

Friends

Quietly we were greeted at the door of the Friends Meeting House
The atmosphere was serene, tranquil, undisturbed
Our first Quaker Meeting, we really didn't know what to expect

A small room with maybe fifteen chairs
A coffee table, the Holy Bible, a vase of fresh flowers and a few leaflets
Ten or twelve people in the room, stillness, not a word spoken

I sat down, closed my eyes, contemplating for some minutes
Reading a leaflet I was informed Quakers have no Minister, no hymns, no readings
However if any one feels the Holy Spirit prompting them to speak – do so

The leaflet also told me that when the Elders shake hands the meeting would end
After maybe twenty minutes a woman stood up, she spoke quite eloquently
I couldn't actually take in what she was saying; I was in a meditative state

What I did understand, now accepting wholeheartedly is the crux of the matter
The bottom line, or should it be the top: GOD IS LOVE
Simple, isn't it. Although heard many times I hadn't grasped this fact

In due time the Elders shook hands, we were then offered coffee
Everyone was friendly, we chatted for half an hour or so
Next Sunday we look forward to seeing our Friends once again

A spiritual awakening?

Sister

About to take her final vows
Not sure, was this a change of heart
Give life to God for eternity
Could she commit to this new start?

Convent life was all she knew
The Sisters filled her with joy
Distant memories of life outside
Would this new life now destroy?

Her love of God, the Holy Book
Was never questioned or in doubt
Her thoughts still wandered to the secular world
Was this a turnabout?

Twelve hours before the awful day
Praying fervently to God above
Received guidance with new direction
Left the Convent for the outside world – the Sisters gave their love

She now ministers at a Hospice
Patients at peace say, she's like a white dove
Through her God's love extends
Touching all with infinite love.

JJ

1st January

New dawn new day new year
Look forward with heart and mind glad
Forget all the sorrow the fear
Our soul our whole being not sad

Rejoice be happy goodwill to all
No expense no cost involved
New beginning no pain, we can start again
This way our troubles are solved

Sins of the past now forgiven
Have faith as we thank God above
All mercy is sent down from Heaven
We move forward, all blessed with His love.

JJ

Ruth

Friendship so wonderful, feelings full of intensity
With Ruth this was always a natural propensity
Treating friends with kindness one could not replicate
From Ruth's heart came love, joy seemed to perpetuate

With no effort Ruth helped others, often unknowingly
Her life will be remembered, as a friendship tapestry
Always helping, Ruth had a special incandescence
Friends ever grateful to receive her unique effervescence

Feelings towards Ruth from all reached adoring
The love they had grew, love was soaring
If something was wrong, Ruth made it right
Ruth's special way, made all see the light

Ruth; one in a million, by our side, our good friend
Not in front not behind, by our side, we'd depend
Ruth died recently; we must now learn to adjust
Each day she is missed, pure friendship, pure trust.

RUTH: Is a Hebrew word meaning "a friend" one who will standby others,
when they are in need.

JJ

P.C.

No longer a lady a woman
I'd give seats up on buses and trains
This habit I've had for a lifetime
But from it I now must refrain

That big metal grate in the road
I've recently had to discover
Is not the name we once knew it by
It's now a person hole cover

When discussing in groups we can't brain storm
It now must be called a thought shower
All smoking is banned we can't say single-manned
Or hello love that's sure out of hand

Touching is definitely out
Touch my elbow would be OK
Touch my back, get the sack, that's harassment
You certainly no longer could stay

Senior Citizen not OAP
Most seem to have high energy
All like to travel the whole world to unravel
And my how they love to SKI.
(Spend kids inheritance)

JJ

Superstition

Don't put shoes on the table, don't cross on the stairs
Don't walk under ladders, but really who cares
Be careful on Friday the thirteenth has been told
Just cross your fingers, go on, be bold

Perhaps wear a rabbit's foot or some white heather
Throw salt over left shoulder to protect, you'll feel better
Wear a bracelet, with seven charms on of course
Touch wood when betting on that well fancied horse

When driving the car a cat's seen on the road
It's black, has nine lives, so onward it goes
Don't sneeze, not on Monday, this could mean danger
Tuesday's OK — you'll kiss a stranger

Sneeze on Sunday, your safety to seek
Or the devil will have you for the rest of the week
So eat something now to ward off evil spirit
Better make sure that garlic is in it.

JJ

Lotto

Fifty pounds a week on the Lottery
Was convinced he'd have a big win
Three years he'd been playing, won five tenners
But like most gamblers he took it right on the chin

The "big one", half a million next Saturday
He felt lucky so doubled his stake
One hundred pounds was his outlay
This weekend he'd be rich, no mistake

Six numbers was all that he needed
The best he thought were 3, 5, 7, 12, 22 and 45
As he watched the results on the telly
His heart skipped a beat, he'd got five

Five numbers, not quite half a million
A big win he'd now receive
But that week saw thousands of winners
Eighty six pounds was his win, did he grieve

There's more chance of getting struck by lightning
Than winning the National Lottery
So he's going outside in the next thunderstorm
To prove if that's true — wait and see.

J J

Beyond

Last night I saw a silver glow
Not flashing fast or beating slow
Above the hill through my bedroom window
Not a star not an aircraft, it remained just so

Pulsating slowly this inexplicable thing
I've just read a book by Stephen King
A UFO was I now seeing
This wasn't made by a human being

I kept my eyes focused I had to keep staring
It seemed to be calling me beckoning daring
What could this be this sight I now witness
My mind is quite stable my body all fitness

I'll open the window get a much clearer view
I need to tell someone this subject's taboo
The wind is now howling it sucks me right out
Up the hill I am carried I shout and I shout

On this object I land a door opens up
I drop down within my mind now is shut
Engines start, building up to a roar
Then…whoosh, off we go, I'll be seen nevermore.

J J

Cockney Speak

He hadn't seen his *trouble* for ages, or the, *saucepans*
Lived in a huge *rat* on his *jack,* always paid the *duke* on time
His *skin* called every week, gave him some lovely *tom* at Christmas
On his birthday bought him two silk *peckhams,* very nice

The *cherry* was getting on his nerves, decided to take him to the *navy*
On with the *mountain,* down the *apples,* into the *jam*
He had *rifle* in his *sky,* might fancy a *ruby* later
With a few glasses of *patsy*

He'd stopped the *oilys* two months ago now just had the occasional *la de*
Loved that with a glass of *gold,* or a cup of *rosie*
Thought he'd treat himself next week, what to get?
Perhaps a new *whistle, St.Louis* and *callards*

Would have to visit the *sherman,* probably draw out a *bag*
Remembering that his *hampsteads* still needed to be sorted

On his way home he called into the *rub,* with the *cherry*
Who should be there, his *trouble* with one of the *saucepans*
She *butchers* at him, still thinking he's got a lovely *boat*

They enjoyed a couple of *pigs* together, then went back to the *rat*
Promising not to *bull* ever again
He was absolutely *lee,* his *trouble* cooked a lovely piece of *duke*
With some excellent *merchant*
Their relationship was not *Calais.*

Rhyming Slang Translation

Apples:	Apples and Pears	Stairs
Bag:	Bag of Sand	Grand (£1000)
Boat:	Boat Race	Face
Bull:	Bull and Cow	Row
Butchers:	Butchers Hook	Look
Calais:	Calais to Dover	Over
Callards:	Callard and Bowser	Trousers
Cherry:	Cherry Hog	Dog
Duke(i):	Duke of Kent	Rent
Duke(ii):	Duke of York	Pork
Gold:	Gold Watch	Scotch (Whisky)
Hampsteads:	Hampstead Heath	Teeth
Jack:	Jack Jones	Own
Jam:	Jam Jar	Car
La De:	La De Da	Cigar
Lee:	Lee Marvin	Starving
Merchant:	Merchant Navy	Gravy
Mountain:	Mountain Goat	Coat
Navy:	Navy Lark	Park
Oilys:	Oily Rag	Fag (Cigarette)
Patsy:	Patsy Kline	Wine
Peckham:	Peckham Rye	Tie
Pigs:	Pigs Ear	Beer
Rat:	Rat and Mouse	House
Rifle:	Rifle Range	Change

Rosie:	Rosie Lee	Tea
Rub:	Rub-a-Dub	Pub
Ruby:	Ruby Murray	Curry
Saucepans:	Saucepan Lids	Kids (Children)
Sherman:	Sherman Tank	Bank
Skin:	Skin and Blister	Sister
Sky:	Sky Rocket	Pocket
St.Louis:	St.Louis Blues	Shoes
Tom:	Tom Foolery	Jewellery
Trouble:	Trouble and Strife	Wife
Whistle:	Whistle and Flute	Suit

Adapt

Yards feet and inches, pounds shillings and pence
Stones, pounds and ounces, all gone, no permanence
Fahrenheit, pints and gallons, systems once taught are no more
Metric, we should all know, to be honest, I'm not sure

Kilometres, fifty pence, centimetres, a two-pound coin
Litres, centigrade and kilos, all this did we purloin
Car manufacturers refer to MPG, road signs are in miles
All must convert eventually – we'll be happy Europhiles.

JJ

Smoke

Walter has a lot to answer
Smoking, I started at the age of ten
Players Weights, Senior Service and Woodbines
I wanted to be one of the men

At fifteen I'd progressed to cheroots and cigars
Havana I thought one of the best
The small ones called Hamlet and Manikin
Were OK but played hell with my chest

When aged nineteen things really did happen
A pipe, this should make me look good
I'd tried rolling my own with Old Holborn and Golden
Like Sherlock a pipe would bring me into adulthood

St.Bruno Three Nuns and Condor
Pipe tobacco I've tried them all
I stopped for two years in the eighties
Without pipe I felt nothing at all

Pipe smoking is now like a hobby
With Swan Vestas a knife and pipe cleaner
My teeth all fell out my lungs I can't shout
Sir Walter — should have had a subpoena.

J J

Haircut

Ladies hairdresser in the High Street is now unisex
No appointments needed just turn up, hear Tracy shout who's next
She said I'll wash it first, turned the chair nearly broke my neck
With new shampoo and shower, thought this really is high-tech

Sitting with my head hung backwards over the sink
The water now is scalding me my scalp has turned bright pink
I sat straight up grabbed a towel, asked what the hell was that?
The "sparks" is due at twelve o'clock what we need is a new thermostat

I got out of the chair and left, I'll return no more
So back to Alberts at the old barbers shop
But he can be such a bore.

JJ

Television

Stayed in last night to watch television
While viewing I had quite a shock
The kids in their room with T.V. no supervision
I thought the "watershed" was at nine o'clock

As the film progressed it got sexy
Gorgeous girls, half naked in bed
As I watched seemed to get apoplexy
After an hour I could really see red

The film should have been a documentary
About new road schemes that would ease the traffic
I continued to watch, seemed elementary
Then it became pornographic

One girl starts cavorting and takes off her bra
Removes stockings then pulls down her pants
I though by her speech she came from the U.S.S.R
But now find she's from Milton, Northants

JJ

Walk

Walkers, ramblers, hikers, I'm not sure what they are
It's Sunday morning once again, at home they leave the car
They walk on tarmac, walk on grass, walk down this narrow road
Looks like they'll conquer Everest, see their heavy load

Trudging down the Dale wearing strange clothes, sticks held within their hands
Strong boots and coloured anoraks, worn on their heads are bands

Then the dreaded knock comes, bang bang, on my front door
"Would you mind terribly if we used your loo — sorry to be a bore."

Perhaps I should say yes and accommodate in every way
But then another knock I'd hear that's why I must say nay.

JJ

Day Off

Work all our life is this a pleasure?
Should we not stop, think more leisure
I reach the station seven thirty in the morning
The wife the kids and the dog, they're still yawning.

I'll miss the train on purpose today
Not to go home I'm going to play
I know what to do the Casino sounds fun
Start playing blackjack may have a good run

Taxi I shout, one pulls up alongside me
The Casino I say — and make it lively
Stop at the Bank must get some cash
Wont be a minute then we'll make a dash

In thirty minutes we're at the Casino
I pay the cab off, feel life a hero
A guy takes my coat says, mind the floor it's still wet
Step right inside place your first bet

I feel lucky today going to win lots of money
Beats work for a living that may sound funny
Blackjack I play the cards are dealt out
Five hundred I place I'm ready to shout

The cards I turn over to my joy and delight
I've got twenty-one gives the dealer a fright
The next bet I loose my bad luck goes on
I'll soon have no money its quarter to one

I leave the Casino at quarter past seven
This day I believed was going to be heaven
When I get home I'll think what I've done
Lost all that money, had little fun

Tomorrow arrives I'm ready to go
Down to the station just like a yo-yo
I now think that work derives some sort of pleasure
I really must learn to combine it with leisure.

JJ

Motorway

Motorway driving becomes quite monotonous
Trucks, cars and caravans can become hazardous
Traffic builds up forming somewhat of a cluster
A crash is heard, we all get in a fluster

Thought of stopping soon to partake of some luncheon
I now see policemen one is wielding a truncheon
Hope there's not going to be any trouble
One looks straight at me his face full of stubble
I'm sure they will sort things, of this I've no doubt
The cars are then moved, a plan well thought out

Traffic's now running again up the road
The lorry in front has an unstable load
It's moving about looks like it will fall
On the rear of the truck it says, "I'm from Senegal"

This driver certainly is a long way from home
Another sign says, "I've visited Rome"
His load today is of pots, terracotta
One could say that his work makes him a globetrotter.

J J

Broad Yorkshire Speak

'Ear all, see all, say nowt;
Eat all, sup all, pay nowt;
An' if ivver tha does owt for nowt, do it fer thissen!

Sh's dahn on peys, an reebub, an'all

'e nivver said nowt neeaways ti neean on 'em

Shift yersens aht o't' rooad!

Wi'ed ter wesh ussens I'cowd watter

Ah s'll bray 'im if 'e dunt gi'e ower

Translation

Hear everything, see everything, say nothing.
Eat everything, drink everything, pay nothing.
And if ever one does something for nothing, one does it for oneself.

She's not keen on peas or rhubarb either

He never said anything at all to anybody

Move out of the way

We had to get washed in cold water

I shall hit him if he doesn't stop

Ford Consul

Five lads, one has his new car
It's Sunday, a trip to Ramsgate
A glorious day, this will be a good outing
On the return journey an horrific head on crash
Alan the driver is killed, people in the other car also die
Will, the front seat passenger sustains serious head injuries
Jim, John and Gurney in the rear are also injured

The scene looks like a battlefield
Bodies strewn across the tarmac road and grass verges
John who was in the middle of the rear seat is still there
He's the only person remaining in the car, he's conscious
The front of the vehicle has gone
Wings, bonnet, wheels, engine, windscreen

A coach pulls up full of passengers
Some get out; one of them comes over to John
Puts his outstretched arm through the rear window
And offers him an untipped John Players cigarette
Saying "You'll be OK mate."

Will eventually made a full recovery, thank God
As did his brother John
Jim and Gurney also regained good health

The mental scars.

J J

What a Life

Brothers Will and John, as children lived in Highgate
Brought up strict Methodists, no grief no strife
Attending Church three times on a Sunday
Dad's the preacher, Mum plays piano
What a life

What a life indeed, it was fantastic
Good neighbours, good friends, such happy days
Go to Parli' Hill Fields and play most Saturdays
Sledge down at speed; fall off, John's finger graze
What a life

Go fishing at the ponds, ride on our bikes
Use our go-kart; we called a cadgey that Dad made
Get home for lunch feed the dog and rabbits
Dads in the garden digging over with the spade
What a life

Mum calls saying "Lunch is ready"
Egg, chips and beans is the order of the day
Will's got more chips than me, not to worry
Lunch now over, up and out again to play
What a life

These memories are but simple, ordinary things
But they mean so very much to me
Remaining firm forever in my mind, whatever happens
Surely this is how a family should be
What a life

Sunday Lunch

Sunday lunch was always at one o'clock
Methodical, routine, but we all enjoyed
The Family round the table together
A time to meet, a time to talk, a time to be close

No More

Now, ping, the microwave oven sounds
Only five minutes, the frozen meal is ready to serve
I'm "on line", I'll eat mine at the desk
I'll take mine to the sitting room, must catch up on the "soaps"
I'm off out now, have mine later

See You.

JJ

A Short Phone Call

Will tomorrow unfold with outstretched wings
Where shall I fly I have no destination
No arrangements no appointments no meetings
All now gone, all is ruined, my life forever changed
It was just a short 'phone call

Start again, explain the reasons why to friends and family
I could tell all, justify my new-found situation
Why should I give reasons no I'll tell it as it is
It was just a short 'phone call

That's it, all done; those who need to know are now informed
Not much comment, said very little really, but they're sorry
Sorry, were they sorry to hear the news maybe shocked
Did they feel pity for me, did they understand my anguish
It was just a short 'phone call

Perhaps I should telephone an old school friend, a good close friend
Talk with him, maybe meet up, have a heart-to-heart
We haven't spoken since last Christmas, I should have been in touch sooner
I ring; his wife says, didn't you know, he passed away last summer
It was just a short 'phone call.

JJ

Despair

Another call, it's 3.27am. Samaritans – can I help you?
Silence, I wait, listen for about thirty seconds
Again quietly say, Samaritans – can I help you?

Still no response, silence, I continue to listen, a minute passes.....If you're
there, perhaps you could tap on the 'phone to let me know. Continuing to
listen faint sounds can be heard, two gentle taps, no one speaks.

This must be very difficult for you, I say, pause – then go on, so glad you felt
strong enough to telephone tonight. I now hear sobbing, this goes on for quite
some time.

Now a voice, sounding very distressed says.... I, I, I've had enough.... I, I, I
can't take any more, it, it, it has to end. Now all I hear is weeping.
I keep listening.

Could you talk with me? Can you tell me what's going on with you? I'm here
for you – I'm here to listen,...my name's John.

I, I, I've taken all the tablets, and I, I, just wanted, wanted, someone to be
with me, to be with me when I die.....Would you like me to call an
ambulance? No, No, No, just, just be there, be there with me.

The caller, still weeping, sobbing, her voice becoming quieter, slurring,
incoherent....
St, sta, stay....just, j, j-just – stay with me.
All is quiet....quiet – no weeping, no sobbing – no dialling tone –
Stillness – silence – calm.

Hello....Hello, I quietly say, no sound....I wait – I wait – minutes, again
softly saying – Hello
Only hushed, silence – I replace the receiver.

3.59am – The telephone rings.........

JJ

Piano Lessons

Miss Cox was my piano teacher
She came every Tuesday to instruct me
While other boys played out in the Avenue
We sat together on the stool, she touched my knee

Her hearing aid made a hissing noise
Miss Cox was a little deaf
She would say, let's start with middle C
Then go on to E. G. B. D. F.

I had trouble remembering all those different notes
Miss Cox said, I'll teach you how, so savour
I know you will learn, always remember that
Every Good Boy Deserves Favour.

JJ

Hazel

Time and again I told her not to walk down the lane alone
She must have got fed up hearing this every time she went out
The bus stop was only a quarter of a mile from home
If you didn't use the lane it was a twenty-minute walk
Keeping to the main road

It was Saturday evening, she was going to a friends house
She promised to be home no later than midnight
Would get a taxi, so no worries
Twelve thirty, still not home, she'll be here soon
Now one o'clock, I am anxious, this has never happened before

One thirty, I telephone her friend
What time did Hazel leave? I ask
Hazel, I haven't seen her this evening
We were out together last night went to the cinema
Why? What's happened?

That was four years ago

God Bless you Hazel

J J

Care

She was feeling low for quite some time
Eventually decided to see the GP
It was more than just feeling fed up
Depression with anxiety was the diagnosis

Her Doctor arranged a date for an assessment
An appointment was made to see a Consultant
The Psychiatric hospital wasn't far away
With some trepidation she duly attended

The Consultant prescribed anti-depressant drugs
Also strongly recommended that she attend the Day Hospital
This would be Monday to Friday the hours 10am – 4pm
Here she would get structure in her life

Group therapy, occupational therapy, lunch, meeting others
All seemed to be going well, having been there six months
Structure was brought back to her life
The drugs seemed to be working well

A meeting was arranged for all patients and staff, then the bombshell
It was announced that the Day Hospital was to close
This will happen within one month
We now have care in the community.

JJ

Joining Forces

Two boys aged eighteen such good friends
Joined the Army, both sent to Iraq
Their parents feeling sad and unhappy
Prayed fervently, please let our kids come back

On arrival the boys went to Baghdad
Each wondered what on earth would transpire
At home both thought themselves lads
Now so different, look around, all is fire

The sound of guns of shells of bombs
Fear engulfed them, no more laughs no smile
Feeling vulnerable in this awful place
Had they to kill, is death worthwhile?

Sniper fire is all around
Where it comes from no one seems to know
A rocket crashes down, hits the boys
Both fall screaming, it's over, bodies glow.

JJ

Down and Out

Leicester Square is where he sleeps most nights, has his own bench
Only a small park, theatre-goers and diners pass by every evening
It's nearly midnight, six benches all occupied, the place stinks
Meths, cider, urine, excrement

The police will no longer take him in, or move him on
The local Mission shelter has banned him
He's been in and out of hospital, detox, many times
They say, "we're unable to do any more for him"
He must help himself

He can't

I'm having dinner with friends tomorrow evening
The restaurant is in Leicester Square

Wonder if I'll see him.

JJ

Tears of Joy

Nine ladies, four gentlemen sitting in high back chairs
Forming a semi-circle in the residents lounge
This was John's first visit as a volunteer befriender
The television was so loud, not one person watching

John approached a lady apprehensively, was she asleep
Her head slightly bowed, all he could see was white hair
He touched her hand gently, she looked up and smiled
Asking, has the programme finished? Are you the new warden?

John replied no to both questions, then introduced himself
If the T.V. isn't being watched shall I turn it off? he asked
Oh yes please do, my name's Hannah, she said in one breath
It's always on, Matron turns it on at breakfast, and it's on all day

John now realised that everyone was staring
He looked round, all eyes still firmly focused on him
Walking to the centre of the room he turned off the T.V.
John told them he would be making a weekly visit, staying two to three hours

Instantly all faces seemed to light up, beaming
Then came a spontaneous round of applause
John didn't feel embarrassed or nervous
A tear trickled down his cheek, a tear of joy.

JJ

Jeff

Jeff had suffered with depression and anxiety for some time
Well at least for the five years I've known him – he's 36 now
We were at a party together last Saturday
He was complaining that he couldn't breathe properly
He had pains in his chest

These were the usual signs that Jeff was having one of his panic attacks
I went outside with him so he could get some fresh air
After a few minutes he seemed much better
Come on I said lets go back in now it's a great party
Jeff's response was, no you go back, and I'll stay here for a while

Half an hour went by, no Jeff, out I go again
There in the front garden laying face down on the grass was Jeff
I run over to him, no sign of breathing, I give mouth-to-mouth, nothing
I rush back to the house, pick up the 'phone, call the emergency services
Within six minutes the ambulance arrives, one of the paramedics rushes over
to Jeff

"I'm sorry", he says.

JJ

Just A Few Words

Friends she'd known for years
Were avoiding her
They knew her husband had died in a car crash
Only four days ago
Why, were they embarrassed?
Not knowing what to say
The funeral had been arranged.

JJ

A.A.

It had taken years, but thank God
I finally did make that call.

JJ

Bewilderment

Waiting for a friend in an empty car park
A cold bright autumn afternoon
It's four o'clock, surprisingly quiet
Not a cloud in sky

Looking ahead by the pay and display meter
I see a schoolboy crouching, holding something up to his face
Is it a handkerchief, perhaps not
It looks like a bag, it is, a plastic bag

What's he doing, the bag is over his mouth and nose
The sides of the bag slowly moving in and out
Do I approach him, ask if he wants help
Do I stay in my car feeling helpless, thanking God it isn't my son

What should I do, I continue to observe the boy
I jump out of the car, run over to him, are you all right I ask
No reply, I put my hand on his shoulder
Suddenly on my own shoulder I feel this strong, vice like grip

Looking up I see this huge man wearing a cap, he has a ruddy complexion
He bellows, what the hell are you doing with my boy
Take your hands off him, I know all about people like you, clear off
I drove home confused, perplexed, and anxious, I did not meet my friend.

JJ

Charles

He entered the Nursing Home last week
Family said they couldn't cope
My good friends Dad, called Charles
A real smashing bloke

I've known him for years, eighty-two he is now
Was surprised they'd sent him away
The Home's right at the top of the hill
He won't like it, but that's where he'll stay

He'd been there a week, I paid a visit
Didn't know how he'd feel, not at all
Reception said, "Charles?" wait a minute
Oh yes, room six, down the hall

I arrived at his door knocking gently
Charles opened the door, smiled at me
How lovely to see you, come in, sit down
Would you like a nice cup of tea?

We talked of past times and present
His hand shaking, while he held his cup
Don't worry said he as he shuffled around
The nurse will come in and wash up

I looked at his hands and his face
He seemed sad, he started to cry
I took hold of his hand, gripping tightly
He said, you know, I'm going to die

Three weeks he told me, that's all I've got left
Alone in this place will I be
When all that I wanted at the end of my days
Was to be with my own family

Charles died, two weeks later
On his own in that room in the home
No colleagues, no friends, no family, Charles died
In that room Charles died alone.

JJ

Self Help

The first cut is the deepest, not so
The second, the third, maybe
A new razor blade, she sat alone
Locked safely in her small bedroom
No hurt, no senses, no pain, no feeling
Release, sweet release, free again
Wait, wait - - - bandages, OK
Today another long sleeved shirt.

J J

What Is The Problem?

The late night Indian take-away looked busy
My friend Michael and I were hungry after working a long hard day
We parked the car round the corner, deciding what to order
"My treat," I said. So it's two chicken madras, pilau rice and naan bread

Time now is eleven thirty, as I enter the shop there's so much noise going on
Five white guys, obviously been drinking, are taunting a black guy
He is being served and just about to pay
This really is terrible, the taunts now get worse

Mocking, chanting monkey like noises, what shall I do
The black guy is handed his bag and given change
He turns to leave, one of the five grabs him
Another pushes him down to the floor
The others then drag him out and start kicking him

I run out to the car, I'm shaking, I feel stick, fearful
My hunger disappears instantly
I scream at Michael, drive off, drive off, quickly!
All right, all right, OK he says – "what's the problem"

Michael's surname is Olubenki

What is the problem?

J J

Neighbour

His new cars' got Sat.Nav. colour screen of course
Top of the range, Jaguar, has paddle gear-shift
D.V.D. C.D. T.V. cream upholstery, special leather

Five bed, Tudor style detached house, just had a new kitchen and bathroom
Marble bath – imported from Italy.
New windows installed four months ago.

The gardens have been landscaped recently
Mahogany pergola, hot spa tub, cobbled terrace
Gas barbecue, massive new greenhouse erected only last week

Wife drives a Porsche 911. Kids at boarding school
Only come home four times a year
He has a good job, something in the money markets, she doesn't work

Don't see them often, say hello that's about it
Very few people visit, usually quiet at weekends
Gardener comes every Saturday the lawns are immaculate.

J J

Unheard

Unheard the cries go on
A child seen at school bruised
He tells his friends he's had a fall again
I'll be all right, he says

Every three or four weeks something is wrong
A cut arm last month
Last summer he had a broken ankle
He said, I was playing football and fell

I speak to him at break time this morning
Having noticed red marks on both his arms
He tells me, as he sobs, that Dad was late in again
He heard shouting downstairs, woke him up

Unheard the cries go on.

JJ

Shopper

I saw that same woman in the supermarket again this morning
Scant groceries in her trolley, but I see two bottles of red wine
And a half bottle of vodka, blue label

Her face, a ruddy complexion, in her forties, kids left home
Husband at the office, she has no job, a lovely house.
Not much to do, few friends, fed up, bored

Each day, a trip to the supermarket, must get the shopping.
A loaf of bread, tea, butter and three bottles

Two years ago she had a Mercedes, top of the range. She no longer drives
Waits in the rain for a bus to go home, can't wait to unload the shopping

Tomorrow she'll be back, has to get the shopping done early
I'm told the store will soon be open 24/7

JJ

Hereafter

Who says the law is right, an innocent man suspended on a rope
Eleven did concur, one disagreed, did he give up hope
The rule of law says he must die, the majority agreed

Eleven men now proved wrong, by them has life been taken
Life is no more, this man is dead, though he is not forsaken
He lived a spiritual life, his soul forgiveness seeks
Believing not in this life, but in eternity

When with us mortal souls his philosophy was such
That life hereafter is all that counts, forgiveness means so much
Eleven men, their conscience seek for life
Their lives will end, forgiveness given, minds now at peace.

JJ

Equal

Not nigger, not coloured not black
Not paki, not asian not afro
"black" or "Asian" may cause offence
We should now say, "visible minority ethnics"

This term allows these communities to be distinguished from others — such as
the Irish and the Greeks — whose members are, according to the new
terminology, "invisible"
Because they tend to be light skinned

Are we all children of God?
Are we all human beings?
Are we visible?
Are we invisible?
We all have a name
We all have a country
Whence we derived our birth and infant nurture

Do we need any of this?

JJ

Outcast

A social outcast I, this has been said somewhat
To take a drink today then tomorrow maybe not
Be sociable, I'm told, join in, have fun
Just one drink today, next day another one

My mind spins with indecision I wish I could be like them
I thought I was many years ago, whisky, I'd drink ten
Time, meetings, dates, they never really mattered
As long as I had a drink in my hand I'd stay 'till I was shattered

Shattered not through tiredness or overwork or toil
But through the drink, I couldn't think at all
Could only think where tomorrow I'd be
Would I get another drink then?
I'm on this alcohol merry-go-round, it just doesn't stop at ten

I have to get off, I have to stop, I know this in my heart
But will I stop just for today, then tomorrow I'll restart
I've had the help from family and friends, I've heard it all before
Should I take it on board, not to be flawed and try to make it law

I will make it my law from this day on never to drink again
Others have tried and tried, most ended up in vein
I am determined to conquer what has become my master, not my friend
This thing called alcohol I will now hate, to the very end.

J J

Winner

Win the day win the fight win the battle
Win the horse race, the lotto, the pools
Win the crossword the scratch card, the bingo
Win the raffle, win the cards win the jewels

Win the cricket win the golf win the snooker
Win the prize, best production at work
Win the cruise win the briefcase win a bottle
Win Win Win, take all doesn't hurt.

J J

Book of Life

You talk about the anomaly of life; you say there is no pattern
Irregularity, deviation from the normal, no fixed order
Should there be routine, methodical each day, life safe, life mundane?
Or a voyage of discovery, stimulating days next page unknown

Exciting, the book of life gives unexpected adventures every day
Not to read again, knowing chapter and verse
Fresh pages fill one with anticipation
Read nine to five, never, always twenty-four hours.

JJ

Dress Sense

Cocktail dress, long evening gown or party frock
A fancy top with smart trousers, what to wear?
The Company was holding its annual dinner dance
This wasn't until six months hence, why get flustered now

The dress worn two years ago was a super little black number
Plunging back, right down to her bottom
She looked terrific, but people would remember
Can't possibly wear that again

Dresses, trousers, tops, shoes, the wardrobe was bursting
Most worn once only, twice at most, if a new venue
A trip to the shops, just to look round was now required
Take the "plastic" just in case

Six hours later, back home, my, what a fabulous gown
Expensive, but looks absolutely stunning
New bag, new shoes is all that's needed
The outfit then complete

The day arrives, lovely hotel, drinks reception at 7 dinner 7.30
We look at the table-plan; we're on table 1, with three other couples
We line up waiting for the Toastmaster to introduce us to our hosts
This done we make our way to the dining room

It all looks so lovely; at the centre of our table are some stunning orchids
There are two couples already at the table, we say hello
Just one couple left to arrive, and that's to our table

Ah, here they come…..Oh my goodness. The identical gown!

Presents

Diamonds, a new car
Or maybe a new house
Eau de Cologne or a night-dress
I'm told it's the thoughts that count.

JJ

Christmas Shopping

Must get all the presents, food shopping as well
This time should be enjoyable, I think its hell
Today

Wind, rain and hail, some sleet and some snow
Getting cold wet and miserable round the shops as I go
Today

Be out for hours, such crowds everywhere
A time of good will — me, I don't care
Today

Trains and buses over crowded, no room move on
The real Christmas Spirit to me, it is gone
Today

Six hours I'm out, gifts for others at Christmas
Will they really appreciate? It's all hit-or-miss
Today.

J J

Artist

Paint touches canvas, hands tremble slightly
Colours unfurling flow, a kaleidoscope
Vermilion dripping unites with flesh

Bristles plough in oil forming grooves
Ochre, pale brownish yellow squelches
Indigo splatters the easel, a break in the clouds

Black, night enters, the picture becomes full of emotion, of self
White, pure white glides the canvas as a train on a bridal gown
Purple, green, wine, vivid colours blend from the mind, from the heart.

JJ

Listen

An ear an ear a listening ear
A mind a listening mind
They talk the talk they walk the walk
But do they ever listen?

Come down in that black hole with me right down
Come down to meet me this must be priority
I will speak will you listen?

Come into my head enter into my feelings please listen, just to me
Don't want your advice or point of view or even observation — just listen

No one else to talk to pour out my heart my soul
No one on this planet, in confidence I need to tell you all, please listen

What I will tell you it might shock, you may abhor my talking
There's not a soul upon this earth I'll tell but you — will you now please listen?

JJ

Hope

Let young people dream, not be dreamless
This ever changing world is unyielding
Dreams, expectations together with desire let flourish

The flame of hope let it burn bright connecting with aspirations
Continuing throughout young lives
Empowering goals, reaching greatness

Let not young dreams or hopes be dashed
Nor let this flame extinguish
Hope continuing, goodness, eminence ultimately will prevail.

JJ

Love

Love like blossom fresh begins
Opening out with intensity, envelops the whole being
Will love flower, become a green leaf, not all are evergreen
Blossom remains not long, leaves discolour and fall
Does love hold fast, ever firm?

Must love be reciprocal, perhaps sometimes one-way
A journey, destination unknown
What is love? divine, eternal, short lived
Love is mystery, definition not discovered, ask anyone.

JJ

Gifts

Walk the land drink in nature
Eyes unable to comprehend the glories
Beauty bestowed pure gifts
Gifts not requested – given freely to all

Indescribable. Wild roses, trees
The very grass beneath feet, green velvet
Birds flying high, fish in the river
Gifts not requested – given freely to all

Gentle rain, sun breaking through the clouds
Colours, all colours, a rainbow, reflections
All seasons, all times, every day
Gifts not requested – given freely to all

J J

Unseen

Rapid as a whirlwind going downstream
Flashing, dashing like diamonds, no deviation
Solitaire or cluster sparkling, hit the granite

Impact, no change, gone always unseen
No clock, no time or date ever remembered
Invisible, will return not seen

Where originates, where terminates, unknown
Will come back, as sure as night follows day
Listen, wait, change course, unable to forget.

J J

Love's Clock

Love's not perpetual motion
Sometimes like an old mantle clock
Stops — what hour, what day, when?

Wind up on Sunday, an eight-day clock
Today is Friday, the clock has stopped
Has love?

She's still in bed, we didn't touch at all
Kept to our own sides, we didn't speak
It's never mentioned, continues

When did it stop, why? There are no answers
No key, no long life battery will re-start
Can't wind up, can't re-wind, it's stopped.

JJ

No Lies

If in doubt speak the truth
Pure unsullied whole truth
No white lies not economical truth no fibs
Genuine, actual, factual, truth

Truth cannot be hidden or covered up
Faithful honesty without mystery, no concealment
Open and forthright no hurt no pain
Truth is good like gentle rain

That is the truth.

J J

Changes

Dark, a cool still wet November morning
Leaves fall gently from the trees
Amber, gold, brown, seasons change
Hearts and minds, do they?
Not long ago the trees stood proud, branches weighed green

Change, decay now seen will vanish
Slowly returning all to former glory
My heart my soul rejoices
The storm the calm blows high and low through life
Trust, endure the changes

J J

United

Friends, good friends, new or old
How do we keep firm grip of this bond?
Our lives in a changing world unfold
Embrace this unknown time

The future beckoning lies before us
Fills us with anticipation and joy
People are all that matter
An absolute belief we should not destroy

An old friend comes to see me
Thirty years since we last met
My heart feels strangely warmed
We greet, our eyes becoming wet

This bond of friendship given to us
Perhaps given from above
Will last for eternity
Forever tinged with love.

JJ

Forever Love

Love floating like feathers reaching out touching ever to remain
No storm, no wind no howling gale can this love dislodge
Through time true hearts love has found, ever to abide
Exquisite, faithful, beautiful, this love will never hide

Love tender, warm, love strong, love true is freely given
In turn received wholeheartedly, this union blessed in heaven
Loves temple, loves sanctuary, loves indistinguishable flame
Burns in hearts, in minds in souls, ever to remain.

JJ

Yesterday

Yesterday, dreams alive, real, explosive
Today, destroyed, flames extinguished
Yesterday, hopes aspirations existing
Today as nothing, optimism vanished

Yesterday excitement, unbounded
Today sorrow, no understanding, tears
Yesterday certainty, laughter burning
Today perplexed, a maze, so many questions.

JJ

Wish

Desire materialistic objects
Or a person, the opposite sex
Maybe the same sex
Something that cannot be
Or hope for the future

I wish you well
In all your undertakings
Is that truth?
Is that wishy-washy?

Real or unreal.

JJ

Benevolence

Kindness wafts around this house
Let it be outside too
No real effort required
An easy routine

Kindness can mean so much
To give and of course receive
Good deeds daily can become habit forming
Such a difference this would make

Let us be just to others
That we may be just to ourselves
This would really bring change
It could be phenomenal.

J J

Killing

If life is worth living how can it be
Wars flourish, life's taken, this is treachery
Will violence end if we all help each other?
No matter where from can we not just say "Brother"

These thoughts are for a much happier place
But the deeds are quite different in fact a disgrace
A soldier is sent to fight in a war
To kill and get killed a thought to abhor

Killing has happened throughout history
Question why, no one knows, a complete mystery
Some day will it stop, forever to end?
Or will life still be taken, our world never mend.

JJ

Life-Span

Three score years and ten
Is this our allotted time?
We could abide much longer
When mind, body and soul are fine
Remain
We're not yet slain
Not yet
Continue on life's road, to travel further on
We pray almighty God
Remaining days are long

Could we stay longer, could we?
The choice it is not ours
Death comes unexpectedly
Coffin strewn with flowers
We expire
Leave situations dire
Always
Now we are as night, ever to remain
No morning dew, no birdsong
Ever seen, ever heard again.

JJ

Day and Night

Days filled with laughter, with joy
Days filled with tears, with sadness
Days filled with sunshine, with brightness
Days filled with rain, with cloud
Days long — Days short
These are the Days

Nights filled with peace, with rest
Nights filled with turmoil, with anxiety
Nights filled with passion, with excitement
Nights filled with fear, with dread
Nights long — Nights short
These are the Nights

J J

With Love

Without love there is nothing at all
A bottomless pit, a canyon too deep and too wide
Bring on love; bring it on, the sun's breaking through
Clouds are gone all is light, no more hide

Be open, unafraid in the light
Carefree we will shine like a beam
Head held high just let love flow
Reaching out, touching all, not a dream

Get the feeling; it is good it is true
With love all is right, all is fair
Accept, let love in let love out
With love, with love we can share

Send a card, we send with love
Receive a gift, we accept with same
With love all things can be different
With love, with love there's no shame.

J J

Unspoken

Words are not needed
How gently hands touch
Feelings of certainty
Sense wholeness so much

Love lifted shadows
No stumble no fall
As Angels, pure light
Love conquering all.

JJ

No Matter

You don't need to tell me where you come from
It doesn't matter
You don't need to tell me what you do for a living
It doesn't matter
You don't need to tell me any of your background
It doesn't matter

We are here together
We are happy
That matters.

JJ

Cecilia

In silk she walks round the great halls
Slim, elegance natural on her befalls
Oh, how I wish that she were mine
Cecilia, floating, she is divine

Her eloquence is matched by none
Soft gentle words from her mouth come
She is to me an English rose
My thoughts, my feelings I must not disclose

Her beauty penetrates both light and dark
Shines as a beacon, the flame from a spark
The effect she has I cannot describe
Cecilia's whole being I imbibe.

CECILIA: From the Latin *caecus*
which means "BLIND"

There is no suggestion that people with this
name are deprived of sight: rather that they are
blind to the wickedness that goes on around them.

J J